Under the Bridge

Lynda Edwards

Level 1

Series Editors: Andy Hopkins and Jocelyn Potter

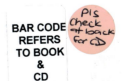

1.1 What's the book about?

Look at Picture A in Activity 1.2. Talk about the picture. What do you think? Then write your answers.

1 Why is the woman sitting there?

....

2 What is in the bags?

....

3 Who is the man?

....

4 Why is he there?

....

1.2 What happens first?

What do you think? Number the pictures, 1–4.

CHAPTER 1

'Go away!'

'Can I ask you some questions?' he said.
Bea didn't want to listen. Questions were always bad.

Bea lived under a **bridge**. She had two bags. In the bags there was a coat, some brown shoes and an old, brown hat. It was very cold in winter. There was a book of photographs too, and a yellow **baby's** dress. These were important to Bea. Why? She didn't remember.

Every day Bea watched the river. She liked watching the people too. A lot of people came under the bridge, but they didn't look at Bea. They usually walked very quickly. They were happy because their **lives** were **different** from hers. They didn't want to see her or talk to her.

Bea didn't like talking, but she liked **singing**. Her songs were from a different life. Sometimes she remembered a house, children and a garden, but she didn't remember very much. Her head was an **empty** room. The bridge was her home now.

bridge /brɪdʒ/ (n) There is a *bridge* across the river.
baby /ˈbeɪbi/ (n) The *baby* is six months old.
life /laɪf/ (n) His *life* is difficult. He hasn't got much money.
different /ˈdɪfərənt/ (adj) My sister and I like *different* things. She meets her friends every evening, but I watch TV.
sing /sɪŋ/ (v, past **sang** /sæŋ/) The Beatles *sang* very well. Their songs are famous.
empty /ˈempti/ (adj) The classroom is *empty*. Where are the students?

'Hello! My name's Martin.' A young man **sat** under the bridge near Bea.

Bea closed her eyes. 'I'm sleeping,' she said. 'Go away!'

The man smiled. 'Can I ask you some questions?' he said.

Bea didn't want to listen. Questions were always bad. She started to sing. 'La – la – la!' she sang **loudly**.

The man waited. Bea opened one eye. The young man had a **nice** smile. She remembered a young man with a nice smile.

'I'm Bea,' she said. 'Why are you sitting under my bridge?'

'You see that house?' He looked at a tall house across the river. It was old with dark windows. Then he looked at Bea. His eyes were very blue and very clever. 'I'm a policeman,' he said. 'I'm watching that house.'

sat /sæt/ (v, past of **sit**) We *sat* in the garden and talked.
loud /laʊd/ (adj) I like *loud* music. My mother is often angry because I play music very *loudly*.
nice /naɪs/ (adj) Your new house is very *nice* – I like it!

CHAPTER 2

'Where is Emily?'

There were policemen in the garden of the tall house.
They moved quietly and looked in the dark windows.

Bea looked at Martin with big eyes. A policeman? She didn't like policemen. They usually had angry faces. 'You can't stay here. Move!' they said to Bea. She always moved, but then she always came back again. This was her bridge.

But this policeman was different. He looked into her eyes. He talked to her. She was a person to him – a person with **feelings**.

'Why?' she asked. 'You've got a job. You can't watch houses. You haven't got time.'

Martin smiled again. 'It is my job!' Bea was a **strange** person, but sometimes there was a clever light in her eyes. 'We don't know, but perhaps there are bad people in that house,' he said quietly. 'Yesterday some men **took** a little girl from her home in town. Her father has a lot of money. Perhaps the men want money from him. This is Em – Emily, the little girl.'

Martin had a picture. The girl had dark hair and a yellow dress and shoes.

---

feeling /ˈfiːlɪŋ/ (n) I'm not ill now, and that's a good *feeling*. I felt ill yesterday, but today I *feel* very happy.
strange /streɪndʒ/ (adj) That's *strange*! The car is empty. Where are our bags?
took /tʊk/ (v, past of **take**) I *took* some money from my bag and went to the ticket office.

Bea looked away. She sat quietly and looked at the river. It moved slowly under the bridge.

'Perhaps they took the little girl to that tall house ...' Martin said.

'No!' Bea said suddenly, very loudly. 'I can't hear you.' Then her eyes went dark and she started to sing again. 'La – la – la!'

Martin looked away. He was wrong. Bea didn't understand. She lived in a **dream**. He started to move away. 'Goodbye, Bea ...'

Bea's hand was suddenly on his coat. 'No,' she said again. 'There aren't any people in that house. It's empty. I watch it.' Bea didn't like talking. It was difficult and her mouth felt strange.

dream /driːm/ (n/v) In my sleep I had a *dream* about a holiday in Senegal. Do people go there on holiday?

'Was there a light in the house, Bea?' Martin asked. 'In the night?'

Bea's head was **full**. She closed her eyes. 'Questions! Questions!' she sang.

'Look, Bea. Look,' Martin said.

There were policemen in the garden of the tall house. They moved quietly and looked in the dark windows.

Bea watched. Where was the little girl? Where was Emily? She had a bad feeling. This was strange for Bea. She didn't have feelings. Sometimes she felt hot or cold, but she never felt happy or unhappy. Now she had a feeling and she didn't like it. She didn't want the feeling. Life was good with no feelings.

But she watched the policemen. Now they were at the door. The house was quiet. The door wasn't strong and it opened. It was dark in the house. The policemen went in.

full /fʊl/ (adj) I walked to school because the bus was *full.*

2.1 Were you right?

Look at your answers to Activity 1.2 on page ii. Then circle the right answers here.

1 Bea lives under the bridge.   (Yes) No

2 She remembers a lot of things about her life.   Yes No

3 Bea doesn't want to talk to Martin.   (Yes) No

4 Martin is a teacher.   Yes (No)

5 The house across the river is old.   (Yes) No

6 Martin is watching the house.   (Yes) No

2.2 What more did you learn?

Write the words in the sentences.

> house   money   empty   angry   dream
> questions   bad   strange

What does Bea think?

1 A lot of policemen are ......*bad*......... .

2 I don't like ......*questions*...... .

3 The old house is ......*empty*...... .

4 This feeling is ......*strang*...... .

What does Martin think?

5 Bea is a ......*angry*...... person.

6 Bea lives in a ......*dream*...... .

7 Emily is in that ......*house*...... .

8 The bad men want ......*money*...... .

2.3 **Language in use**

Look at the sentences on the right.
Then circle the right words in these
sentences.

> A young man sat **under** the
> bridge **near** Bea.
> They moved quietly and
> looked **in** the dark windows.

1 Bea looked *on* / *at* the house.

2 Bea's life was different *of* / *from* Martin's life.

3 Martin had a picture *of* / *to* Emily.

4 The men wanted money *of* / *from* her father.

5 The bags were important *at* / *to* Bea.

6 Martin talked *at* / *to* Bea.

2.4 **What happens next?**

What is going to happen? Write ✓ or ✗.

CHAPTER 3

'Can we look in your house?'

*Now she remembered an important thing. She put her hand
on Martin's coat again. 'I was in there today,' she said.*

Martin went across the bridge to the old house. A policeman came out. 'Emily?' Martin asked.

'No,' the policeman said. 'It's empty.'

Martin and the policemen went to every house in the street. The doors opened and the policemen asked the same question: 'Can we look in your house?' They looked, but they didn't find the little girl.

'Perhaps this is the wrong road,' Martin said. Where was Emily? Did Bea know? She watched the river and the houses every day. Martin went and sat down under the bridge again.

'She isn't there,' he said. 'We were wrong.'

'I know.' Bea started to like this young man. His eyes smiled.

Suddenly her head felt light. Usually it felt very heavy and full of strange noises. Sometimes she remembered things and it felt light. Now she remembered an important thing. She **put** her hand on Martin's coat again. 'I was in there today,' she said.

Martin waited. What did Bea know?

'Sometimes I go in the house because it's cold here,' she said.

'It was cold this morning,' Martin said.

'I went there. There wasn't a little girl. No bad people.' Bea's head was heavy again. She closed her eyes.

Martin waited, but Bea was quiet. He took some **chocolate** from his coat. 'Bea? Here's some chocolate.'

Bea opened an eye again. 'Mmm,' she said. Bea loved chocolate. She took it and put some in her mouth. It was good. Then she

---

put /pʊt/ (v, past of **put**) He *put* a bottle of water on the table.
chocolate /ˈtʃɒklɪt/ (n) I eat a lot of *chocolate*. I love it, but it isn't good for me!

opened her bag. There was the baby's dress.

Martin smiled. 'That's nice!' he said.

'Look,' Bea said and she took out the book of photographs. 'Pictures.'

Martin opened the book. There was a picture of a beautiful young woman and a little girl. He looked at Bea. The young woman had the same eyes. 'Is that you?' he asked.

Bea smiled. 'I don't know,' she said quietly and she looked in her bag again. Suddenly she put a hand to her mouth. 'Oh!' she said. Her face was white.

'What is it, Bea?' Martin asked.

Bea slowly took two small, yellow shoes from the bag. She remembered. 'I took them. For my little girl. They were in that tall house.'

CHAPTER 4

'It was only a dream.'

*There was a room with a lot of lights and people. There was
music too, and a little girl in a yellow dress danced.*

'We were right,' Martin said. 'The bad people were in the
house with Emily. They came and then they went again.
Perhaps they know about the police.'

There were **tears** in Bea's eyes. She put the shoes and the dress
near her face. She remembered a little girl in the dress, her little girl.
Were the tears for that little girl or for Emily? She didn't know.

Martin put his hand on Bea's. 'Bea, we want to find Emily. My
men are going to watch the house again at night. Perhaps the bad
people are going to come back with Emily. Can you watch it too?'
Then Martin went away.

Night came. It was dark under the bridge, but there were lights in
the road. There was a car near the tall house. It was a police car. But
the road was empty.

Bea wanted to sleep. Her head
was full of strange pictures, but she
didn't want them. She wanted her
old, quiet life. But she wanted to
find Emily too. She looked at the
tall house. It had a big **roof**. Every
house in the street had a big roof and
some houses had windows there. In
one window there was a light and a
young man sat with a book.

tear /tɪə/ (n) The woman was unhappy. There were *tears* in her eyes.
roof /ruːf/ (n) There was a small animal on the *roof* of the house.

Bea had a new picture in her head now. There was a room with a lot of lights and people. There was music too, and a little girl in a yellow dress danced. 'Look, Mama!' she said to Bea. 'New shoes!' Then the picture went and Bea was under the bridge again.

Suddenly her eyes went to the tall, dark house. Why did she look there? Was there a person? The windows were dark but there, up in the roof, there was … Bea looked and looked. It was difficult in the dark. What was it? Bea's mouth opened. It was a small, white face. It was the face of a little girl. Bea closed her eyes and waited. Then she opened them. There was no face, no little girl. It was only a dream. Bea closed her eyes again, this time for sleep.

3.1 Were you right?

Look at your answers to Activity 2.4. Then think about these sentences.
What happens first? Write the numbers 1–9.

a [6] A police car watches the house.

b [ ] Bea takes the yellow shoes from the kitchen.

c [2] The policemen don't find Emily.

d [5] Martin gives some chocolate to Bea.

e [ ] Bea sees a face at the window.

f [1] Bea goes to the house.

g [ ] Bea sees a young man near a window.

h [ ] Bea has a dream.

i [ ] Martin looks at Bea's photographs.

3.2 What more did you learn?

Match the sentences on the left with sentences on the right.

1 Bea sometimes goes into the house.

2 Bea opens one eye.

3 Bea's face is white.

4 Bea puts her hand on Martin's coat.

5 There are tears in Bea's eyes.

6 Bea looks at the window.

7 Bea closes her eyes.

a She sees a person.

b She wants to talk.

c She remembers her child.

d She wants to sleep.

e She feels cold.

f She remembers the shoes.

g She likes chocolate.

3.3 **Language in use**

Look at the sentences on the right.
What are sentences 1–5 about?

> '**She** isn't there.'   [**Emily**]
>
> **It** was only a dream. [**The face**]

1 '**That**'s nice!'   ....a picture.........

2 'Is **that** you?'   ....

3 'I took **them**.'   ...in the house.....

4 '**They** came and **they** went again.'   ....

5 'Can you watch **it** too?'   ....

3.4 **What happens next?**

What do you think? Circle the right answers.

1 The policemen see the bad man in the house.   Yes No

2 Emily runs across the bridge.   Yes No

3 Bea falls into the water.   Yes No

4 Bea lives with Martin's family.   Yes No

5 Emily's father gives some money to Bea.   Yes No

6 Martin finds Bea's daughter.   Yes No

CHAPTER 5

'She's in the house!'

'No!' the man in the water said. 'I can't swim!'
'Good,' said Bea.

'Good morning, Bea,' Martin said. It was early. It was a nice day. The sun was hot, but it wasn't hot under the bridge. He sat down.

Bea smiled. She liked the sun and she liked Martin. She took the book of photographs out of her bag. She wanted to look at the pictures again with her new friend. They looked at a picture of a big house.

'Did you live there?' Martin asked.

'Perhaps,' Bea said. She started to sing again. Martin listened.

Today Bea's song was beautiful. It was a slow love song. Martin remembered the song. Perhaps his mother sang it to him.

Bea looked at the dress and the yellow shoes. 'I dreamed about my little girl,' she said quietly. 'She danced and I sang a song for her.'

'Did she like the song?' Martin asked.

'Yes. Then it went dark again. Her face was at the window.' Bea

was unhappy. There were tears on her face.

'Where was the window in your dream, Bea?'

'Up there, in the roof.' Martin looked across the river. The window was dark, but ... He looked again. What was that on the window? Yes – there were some letters. Martin took his phone. 'Quick – she's in the house – in the roof!'

Bea watched. Martin and the policemen went into the house quickly. They didn't see a man in the garden, but Bea did. The man came out of a window and went across the garden and then across the bridge. His legs moved quickly. His face was very red. He came under Bea's bridge, but he didn't see Bea. She was very quiet. Was this the man? Did this man take little Emily?

Suddenly Bea had a new feeling. She was angry. This was a very bad man. He took children. The man came near Bea and she put her foot in front of him. He didn't see it and he went into the water. There was a loud noise. The policemen came out of the house and looked at the river.

'No!' the man in the water said. 'I can't swim!'

'Good,' Bea said.

The policemen took the man from the river. Then they put him in a police car. The policemen took the man away in a police car.

Martin came out of the tall house. There was a little girl with him. She had dark hair. She looked across the river at Bea and smiled.

16

CHAPTER 6

'I know your name.'

She had a family. People loved her. She put her hand on Martin's.
'I went away,' she said quietly. 'I remember now.'

Martin was happy. Emily was at home with her mother and father. The man was at the police station. But Martin wanted to know about Bea. The bridge wasn't a good place for her. Was there a home for Bea too? Martin remembered the photographs and her songs. Then he went on his **computer** and he looked at some old newspapers.

'Yes!' he said after a lot of work. There was a picture of a famous young woman and a little girl in a yellow dress – the picture in Bea's book! There was a story with the picture: *Where is Beatrice?*

computer /kəmˈpjuːtə/ (n) I do my homework on my new *computer*.

Bea looked up at Martin. 'Hello!' she smiled. 'How is Emily?'

Martin sat down. 'She's well. She says "thank you". The police went into the house and she was in a small room in the roof. She was in the house. We didn't know. But you did.'

Bea's face went red and she looked at the river.

'Bea,' Martin said quietly. 'I know your name.'

Bea didn't understand. 'Yes. I'm Bea.'

'Your name is Beatrice. And you were a singer. A good singer.'

'I like singing,' Bea said.

'And you had a family and a daughter. Her name was Gr–'

'Grace,' Bea said quickly. There was a light in her eyes. 'Her name was Grace. I remember.'

'There was a car **accident**. You weren't well. You didn't remember things. Then one day you weren't in your room. Your family looked for you. The police looked for you. But they didn't find you.'

Bea's head felt very light. She had a family. People loved her. She put her hand on Martin's. 'I went away,' she said quietly. 'I remember now.'

accident /ˈæksɪdənt/ (n) Two cars had an *accident* in the road near our house.

Martin felt tears in his eyes. 'Look, Bea – Beatrice.' A car stopped near the bridge. A young woman came out. She was tall and beautiful and her dress was yellow.

'Mama?' she said and she put out her hand.

Bea looked at the woman and she had a good, happy feeling. There was love in her eyes. Then she looked at Martin. 'Thank you,' she said.

And Bea went away from the bridge, away from her two bags. She went to her new life.

Martin watched her. 'No, Bea,' he said. 'Thank *you*.' And he looked at the tall, old house with the dark windows. It was empty again.

Work with two or three friends.

1 | **Student A** | You are a person in the story. Answer questions.

Students B–D | Ask questions about the life of the person in the story.

What time do you get up?

What do you do every morning?

2 **You are going to make a TV film of the story, in English or in your language. Talk about these questions:**

a Who are going to play the people in the story?

b Where are you going to film the story?

c Are people going to like it? Why (not)?

Bea's story is in the newspaper. Write the article.

New life for famous singer

Do you remember Beatrice? She was a famous singer. She was in a bad car accident and ......

Project *Do you remember ...?*
Bea had an accident. She doesn't remember things about her life.

1 **Do you remember things? Which of these people is you? Talk to your friends.**

A I always remember things.

B I listen to music and I remember things.

C I don't remember people's names.

D I remember important things.

E I remember telephone numbers.

G I write things down and then I remember them.

2 **People often have photographs in a book or on their computer. What are these photographs of?**

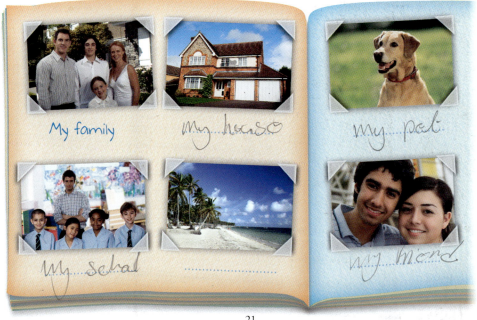

My family

My house

my pet

My school

....

my friend

3 **Bring a photograph to school and talk about it with your friends.**

   a What is the place?   **c** When was it?

   b Who are the people?   **d** Why do you like the photograph?

4 **Write a questionnaire for your friends. Write questions. Then ask three or four people and write short answers. How much do they remember? What do you learn about your friends?**

QUESTIONNAIRE

What do you remember about ...

1 your first teacher?

2 your first year at school?

3 your first book?

4

5

6

7

8

9

10